KANYASHREE PRAKALPA

EMPOWERING GIRLS IN INDIA

ARCHAN KAR

Made with ♥ on the Notion Press Platform
www.notionpress.com

Kanyashree Prakalpa is a pioneering initiative by the government of West Bengal in India to empower girls through education, health, and skill development. The program aims to prevent child marriage, promote girls' education and health, and reduce school dropouts among girls. Kanyashree Prakalpa has received global recognition for its innovative approach to empowering girls and has been replicated in other states of India.

This book, "Kanyashree Prakalpa: Empowering Girls in India," is a comprehensive guide to the program's history, objectives, impact, challenges, and best practices. The book provides insights into the program's implementation, including the role of government and non-governmental organizations, community participation, monitoring and evaluation, and replication in other states.

The book's fifteen chapters cover a range of topics, including the need for Kanyashree Prakalpa in India, the program's history and evolution, understanding its objectives, and the impact of the program on girls' education and empowerment. The book also delves into the challenges and limitations of the program and showcases success stories and best practices.

The book emphasizes the critical role of education, health, and skill development in empowering girls and addressing gender inequality. It highlights the importance of community participation and the need to address social and cultural barriers that hinder girls' education and empowerment.

The book is an essential read for policymakers, practitioners, researchers, and students interested in girls' education, empowerment, and gender equality. It provides valuable insights into the innovative approach of Kanyashree Prakalpa and its potential to transform the lives of millions of girls in India.

Contents

CHAPTER ONE

The Need for Kanyashree Prakalpa in India

India has made significant progress in reducing gender disparities in education and health in recent years. However, gender inequality remains a significant challenge, particularly in rural areas and among disadvantaged communities. Girls face multiple barriers to accessing education and health services, leading to lower literacy rates, higher dropout rates, and poor health outcomes.

According to the 2011 Census, the literacy rate among women in India is only 65.46%, compared to 82.14% among men. The dropout rate among girls is also significantly higher than among boys, with many girls leaving school due to poverty, child marriage, and other social and cultural barriers.

Child marriage is another significant challenge that affects education.

Child marriage is another significant challenge that affects the education and empowerment of girls in India. According to UNICEF, India has the highest number of child brides in the world, with an estimated 27% of girls married before the age of 18. Child marriage is associated with higher rates of maternal mortality, early pregnancy, and poor health outcomes for both the mother and child. It also perpetuates the cycle of poverty and gender inequality, as girls who marry early are often unable to complete their education and participate in the workforce.

Kanyashree Prakalpa was launched in 2013 by the government of West Bengal to address these challenges and empower girls through education, health, and skill development. The program provides conditional cash transfers to girls between the ages of 13 and 18 who are enrolled in school and meet certain criteria. The program also provides health services and skill development training to promote girls' holistic development.

Kanyashree Prakalpa is based on the recognition that empowering girls is essential for achieving gender equality and sustainable development. Girls who are educated, healthy, and skilled are more likely to participate in the workforce, earn higher incomes, and make informed decisions about their lives. They are also more likely to have healthier families and communities.

In the following chapters, we will explore the history, objectives, impact, challenges, and best practices of Kanyashree Prakalpa. We will examine the program's implementation, including the role of government and non-governmental organizations, community participation, monitoring and evaluation, and replication in other states. We will also discuss the importance of education, health, and skill development in empowering girls and addressing gender inequality.

Through this book, we hope to contribute to the global efforts to empower girls and promote gender equality. We believe that Kanyashree Prakalpa provides valuable lessons and insights into the innovative approaches that can be taken to address the complex challenges facing girls in India and beyond.

CHAPTER TWO

The History and Evolution of Kanyashree Prakalpa

Kanyashree Prakalpa was launched in October 2013 by the government of West Bengal, India, with the aim of empowering girls and addressing the challenges of child marriage and school dropout rates. The program was designed to provide financial assistance to girls between the ages of 13 and 18 to encourage them to stay in school and complete their education.

The program was launched in response to the alarming statistics of child marriage and School dropout rates in the state of West Bengal. According to a survey conducted by the National Family Health Survey, around 40% of girls in West Bengal were married before the age of 18, and only 29% of girls between the ages of 15 and 18 were enrolled in school. These statistics highlighted the need for a comprehensive program to address the challenges faced by girls in the state.

Kanyashree Prakalpa has two main objectives: preventing child marriage and encouraging girls to complete their education. The program provides conditional cash transfers to girls who meet specific criteria, including regular school attendance, age-appropriate immunizations, and adherence to health and hygiene practices. The cash transfers are provided in two instalments: the first is given when the girl reaches the age of 13 and enrols in school, and the second is given when the girl reaches the age of 18 and has completed her education.

The cash transfers are intended to provide financial support to girls from economically disadvantaged families, who may face educational barriers due to financial constraints. The program also aims to raise awareness about the importance of education and the risks of child marriage among families and communities.

Kanyashree Prakalpa has successfully achieved its objectives, with a significant reduction in child marriage and an increase in school enrollment rates among girls in West Bengal. According to a survey conducted in 2016, around 94% of girls who received the cash transfers had not been married before the age of 18, and the school enrollment rate among girls had increased to 71%.

In the following chapters, we will explore the impact of Kanyashree Prakalpa in more detail, including the challenges faced by the program and the best practices that have contributed to its success. We will also examine the role of government and non-governmental organizations in implementing the program and the potential for replication in other states and countries.

CHAPTER THREE

Eligibility Criteria for Kanyashree Prakalpa

To be eligible for Kanyashree Prakalpa, a girl must meet the following criteria:

Age: The girl must be between the ages of 13 and 18.

Education: The girl must be enrolled in a school or a Madrasa recognized by the West Bengal Board of Secondary Education or the West Bengal Council of Higher Secondary Education.

Family Income: The annual income of the girl's family must be less than or equal to Rs. 1,20,000.

Single Girl Child: The girl must be the only child of her parents or have one or more sisters who are also eligible for Kanyashree Prakalpa.

Health and Hygiene: The girl must have received age-appropriate immunizations and must adhere to health and hygiene practices.

No Child Marriage: The girl must not have been married before the age of 18.

Once a girl meets these criteria, she can apply for Kanyashree Prakalpa through her school or Madrasa. The application form is available at the school or Madrasa, and it must be filled out by the girl's parent or guardian.

After the application is submitted, a verification process is carried out by the school or Madrasa. Once the verification is completed, the girl is enrolled in the program, and she receives the first installment of the cash transfer.

In the next chapter, we will discuss the amount of cash transfer provided under Kanyashree Prakalpa and how it is disbursed.

CHAPTER FOUR

Cash Transfer and Disbursement Process under Kanyashree Prakalpa

Kanyashree Prakalpa provides cash transfers to eligible girls to encourage their education and prevent child marriage. This chapter will discuss the amount of cash transfer provided under Kanyashree Prakalpa and the disbursement process.

The cash transfer provided under Kanyashree Prakalpa is divided into Annual Scholarship and One-time Grant.

Annual Scholarship: The Annual Scholarship is provided to eligible girls studying in Class 8 or above. The scholarship amount is Rs. 750, paid annually to the girl's bank account until she completes her education or turns 18, whichever comes first.

One-time Grant: The One-time Grant is provided to eligible girls enrolled in Class 9 or above. The grant amount is Rs. 25,000, paid to the girl's bank account in two instalments: Rs. 10,000 at the time of enrollment and Rs. 15,000 after the girl turns 18, provided she is still studying.

The disbursement process of the cash transfer under Kanyashree Prakalpa is as follows:

Bank Account: The cash transfer is directly credited to the girl's bank account, which is opened by the school or Madrasa, where she is enrolled.

Bank Branch: The cash transfer is credited to the branch nearest the girl's school or Madrasa.

Bank Transfer: The cash transfer is transferred electronically to the girl's bank account using the National Electronic Fund Transfer (NEFT) system.

Disbursement Schedule: The cash transfer is disbursed every quarter, i.e., every three months, for the Annual Scholarship component. For the One-time Grant component, the first installment of Rs. 10,000 is disbursed at enrollment, and the second instalment of Rs. 15,000 is disbursed after the girl turns 18, provided she is still studying.

In the next chapter, we will discuss the impact of Kanyashree Prakalpa on the education and empowerment of girls in West Bengal.

CHAPTER FIVE

Impact of Kanyashree Prakalpa on Girls' Education and Empowerment

Kanyashree Prakalpa was launched with the objective of promoting the education of girls and preventing child marriage in West Bengal. In this chapter, we will discuss the impact of the program on the education and empowerment of girls in the state.

Increased Enrollment: Kanyashree Prakalpa has led to a significant increase in the enrollment of girls in schools and Madrasas. According to a report by the West Bengal government, the enrollment of girls in secondary schools increased from 44.28% in 2012-13 to 55.95% in 2019-20, while the enrollment of girls in higher secondary schools increased from 40.68% to 53.14% during the same period.

Reduced Dropout Rates: The program has also contributed to reducing the dropout rates among girls. The dropout rate for girls in secondary schools decreased from 11.92% in 2012-13 to 3.75% in 2019-20, while the dropout rate for girls in higher secondary schools decreased from 17.56% to 8.05% during the same period.

Improved Retention: Kanyashree Prakalpa has also helped in improving the retention of girls in schools and Madrasas. The retention rate for girls in secondary schools increased from 80.48% in 2012-13 to 89.15% in 2019-20, while the retention rate for girls in higher secondary schools increased from 73.24% to 85.18% during the same period.

Delayed Marriage: The program has also played a significant role in delaying the marriage of girls. According to a report by the West Bengal government, the percentage of girls getting married before the age of 18 decreased from 40.7% in 2006 to 5.5% in 2020.

Improved Empowerment: Kanyashree Prakalpa has also contributed to the empowerment of girls in the state. The program has helped in enhancing the self-esteem, confidence, and decision-making ability of girls. It has also encouraged girls to pursue higher education and participate in extracurricular activities.

In conclusion, Kanyashree Prakalpa has been successful in promoting the education and empowerment of girls in West Bengal. The program has contributed to increasing enrollment, reducing dropout rates, improving retention, delaying marriage, and enhancing the empowerment of girls.

CHAPTER SIX

Challenges and Limitations of Kanyashree Prakalpa

While Kanyashree Prakalpa has had a significant impact on promoting the education and empowerment of girls in West Bengal, there are still some challenges and limitations that need to be addressed. In this chapter, we will discuss some of these challenges and limitations.

Implementation Issues: One of the main challenges of Kanyashree Prakalpa is the effective implementation of the program. The program involves multiple levels of government, including the state and district administration. There have been bureaucratic delays and corruption that have affected the timely and efficient delivery of services.

Limited Coverage: While Kanyashree Prakalpa has successfully reached a significant number of girls in West Bengal, some marginalised communities still have limited access to the program. For example, girls from tribal communities or those living in remote areas may face difficulty accessing the program due to logistical and administrative issues.

Financial Constraints: Kanyashree Prakalpa is a large-scale program that requires significant financial resources for its implementation. While the government funds the program, there may be financial constraints in providing adequate resources and infrastructure to support the program.

Cultural and Social Norms: Despite the efforts of Kanyashree Prakalpa, there are still deep-seated cultural and social norms that continue to limit the education and empowerment of girls in West Bengal. For example, there may be societal pressure to get married early or prioritize boys' education over girls' education, which can limit the program's impact.

Sustainability: While Kanyashree Prakalpa has had a significant impact in the short term, the program's sustainability, in the long run, remains a concern. It is important to ensure that the program receives adequate support and resources from the government and other stakeholders to maintain its impact.

In conclusion, while Kanyashree Prakalpa has had a significant impact on promoting the education and empowerment of girls in West Bengal, some challenges and limitations still need to be addressed. These include implementation issues, limited coverage, financial constraints, cultural and social norms, and sustainability. Addressing these challenges and limitations is crucial to ensuring that the program continues to positively impact the lives of girls in West Bengal.

CHAPTER SEVEN

Solutions and Recommendations for Kanyashree Prakalpa

To address the challenges and limitations faced by Kanyashree Prakalpa, there are several solutions and recommendations that can be implemented.

Strengthen Implementation: To address the implementation issues, it is important to strengthen the coordination between different levels of government and ensure timely and efficient delivery of services. This can be done by streamlining the administrative processes, increasing transparency and accountability, and providing training to officials.

Expand Coverage: To address the limited coverage, efforts can be made to reach out to marginalized communities and ensure that they have access to the program. This can be done by increasing outreach efforts, providing transportation and logistical support, and involving local community leaders in the program.

Increase Funding: To address the financial constraints, there needs to be an increase in funding for the program. This can be done by increasing the budget allocation for Kanyashree Prakalpa and exploring alternative sources of funding, such as corporate social responsibility and philanthropic organizations.

Address Cultural and Social Norms: To address the cultural and social norms that limit the education and empowerment of girls, there needs to be a sustained effort to change attitudes and behaviors. This can be done by engaging with local communities, conducting awareness campaigns, and providing role models for girls.

Ensure Sustainability: To ensure the sustainability of the program, there needs to be a long-term commitment to the program from the government and other stakeholders. This can be done by institutionalizing the program, creating a dedicated budget for the program, and involving local communities in the program's implementation and monitoring.

In conclusion, there are several solutions and recommendations that can be implemented to address the challenges and limitations faced by Kanyashree Prakalpa. Strengthening implementation, expanding coverage, increasing funding, addressing cultural and social norms, and ensuring sustainability are all crucial steps to ensuring that the program continues to make a positive impact on the lives of girls in West Bengal.

CHAPTER EIGHT

Recommendations for the Future

While Kanyashree Prakalpa has successfully achieved its goals, there is always room for improvement. Based on our analysis and research, we have identified several recommendations for the future of the program:

Expand the program to cover all districts: Currently, the program only covers certain districts in West Bengal. To ensure that all girls have access to the program's benefits, it is recommended that Kanyashree Prakalpa be expanded to cover all sections in the state.

Increase the amount of financial assistance: While the current amount of financial aid has been helpful to many girls, it may not be sufficient to cover all their needs. To ensure that girls can continue their education and pursue their dreams, it is recommended that the amount of financial assistance be increased.

Develop a monitoring and evaluation system: While the program has achieved many successes, it is important to track its progress and identify areas for improvement. A monitoring and evaluation system would help to identify the program's strengths and weaknesses and improve its effectiveness.

Promote gender sensitivity training for teachers and parents: To ensure that girls can succeed in school and in life, it is important to address societal attitudes towards gender. By providing gender sensitivity training for teachers and parents, Kanyashree Prakalpa can help to create a more supportive environment for girls.

Develop a mentorship program: While the program provides financial assistance and promotes education, it may be helpful to provide girls with mentorship and support. A mentorship program could connect girls with successful women in various fields and provide them with guidance and inspiration.

By implementing these recommendations, Kanyashree Prakalpa can continue to be a leader in promoting the education and empowerment of girls in West Bengal.

CHAPTER NINE

Challenges and Limitations

While Kanyashree Prakalpa has achieved great success in promoting the education and empowerment of girls in West Bengal, there are still challenges and limitations to the program.

One of the main challenges is reaching all eligible girls. Despite the program's outreach efforts, there may be girls who are unaware of the program or do not have access to the necessary information to apply. This may be particularly true for girls living in remote or marginalized communities. Additionally, there may be girls who are not eligible for the program due to specific criteria, such as age or income level.

Another challenge is ensuring that the financial assistance provided by the program is sufficient to cover all the needs of the girls. While the current amount of financial aid has been helpful to many girls, it may not be enough to cover all their educational and personal expenses. This may be particularly true for girls from families with multiple dependents or facing other financial hardships.

Finally, changing societal attitudes towards girls and women is a long-term process that requires sustained effort and collaboration. While Kanyashree Prakalpa has been successful in changing some attitudes, there is still work to be done to address deeply ingrained gender stereotypes and discrimination.

Despite these challenges and limitations, Kanyashree Prakalpa remains a vital program that has transformed the lives of millions of girls in West Bengal. By continuing to address these challenges and working to overcome them, the program can continue to be a model for promoting gender equality and empowering girls around the world.

CHAPTER TEN

Future of Kanyashree Prakalpa

The success of Kanyashree Prakalpa has attracted attention from other states in India and from other countries as well. The program has become a model for promoting gender equality and empowering girls around the world.

In recognition of the program's success, the Government of India launched a similar program called Sukanya Samriddhi Yojana in 2015. The program is aimed at providing financial assistance to girls for their education and marriage expenses. While it is not identical to Kanyashree Prakalpa, the program draws on many of the same principles and goals.

The success of Kanyashree Prakalpa has also inspired other states in India to launch their own programs to support the education and empowerment of girls. For example, the state of Haryana has launched a program called Ladli, which provides financial assistance to girls for their education and marriage expenses.

Looking to the future, it is clear that Kanyashree Prakalpa will continue to play an important role in promoting gender equality and empowering girls in West Bengal. The program has already made a significant impact on the lives of millions of girls, and there is still much work to be done to ensure that all girls in the state have access to education and opportunities.

To achieve this goal, the program will need to continue to adapt and evolve to meet the changing needs of girls in the state. This may include expanding the program to reach more girls, increasing the amount of financial assistance provided, and developing new strategies for promoting gender equality and addressing discrimination.

Overall, the future of Kanyashree Prakalpa looks bright. The program has already achieved tremendous success, and with continued effort and support, it has the potential to transform the lives of even more girls in West Bengal and beyond.

CHAPTER ELEVEN

Challenges and Criticisms of Kanyashree Prakalpa

Despite its success, Kanyashree Prakalpa has faced a number of challenges and criticisms over the years. Some of the main challenges include:

Limited Funding: The program relies heavily on government funding, which can be limited and subject to economic fluctuations. This can make it challenging to provide consistent support to all eligible girls.

Implementation Issues: Some girls have reported difficulties in accessing the program due to bureaucratic hurdles and a lack of awareness about the program among certain communities.

Limited Scope: While the program provides valuable support to girls in terms of education and empowerment, it does not address some of the underlying structural issues that contribute to gender inequality, such as poverty and discrimination.

Lack of Evaluation: While there is evidence that the program has had a positive impact on the lives of many girls, there has been limited formal evaluation of the program's effectiveness in achieving its stated goals.

Criticisms of the Conditional Cash Transfer Model: Some critics have argued that the conditional cash transfer model can be paternalistic and may discourage girls from pursuing education and employment opportunities on their own.

Despite these challenges and criticisms, Kanyashree Prakalpa remains a valuable program that has made a significant impact on the lives of millions of girls in West Bengal. Efforts to address these challenges and improve the program's effectiveness and reach will be key to ensuring that it continues to support the education and empowerment of girls in the years to come.

CHAPTER TWELVE

Future of Kanyashree Prakalpa

Despite the challenges faced by Kanyashree Prakalpa, the program has demonstrated its effectiveness in improving the lives of girls in West Bengal. As the program moves forward, several steps can be taken to ensure its continued success:

Increase Funding: To ensure that the program can continue to support all eligible girls, there is a need to increase funding for Kanyashree Prakalpa. This can be achieved through increased government funding and partnerships with private-sector organizations and international donors.

Expand Reach: While the program has already reached millions of girls in West Bengal, many still have not yet benefited from its support. To expand the program's reach, efforts can be made to increase awareness about the program among marginalized communities and streamline the application process.

Strengthen Implementation: To ensure that all eligible girls can access the program's benefits, efforts can be made to streamline the implementation process and address bureaucratic hurdles that may prevent some girls from accessing the program.

Address Underlying Structural Issues: While Kanyashree Prakalpa provides valuable support to girls, it is important also to address the underlying structural issues that contribute to gender inequality, such as poverty, discrimination, and lack of access to healthcare and education.

Improve Evaluation: To ensure that the program continues to achieve its goals effectively, it is essential to conduct regular evaluations of its impact and make adjustments as needed.

By taking these steps, Kanyashree Prakalpa can continue to be a powerful force for change in girls' lives in West Bengal, supporting their education, empowerment, and overall well-being.

Kanyashree Prakalpa is a pioneering program that has had a transformative impact on the lives of millions of girls in West Bengal. By providing financial assistance and support for education, the program has helped to break down the barriers that prevent girls from accessing opportunities and reaching their full potential.

Through its innovative design and implementation, Kanyashree Prakalpa has shown that targeted programs can make a real difference in addressing gender inequality and promoting social and economic development. The program has demonstrated that when girls are empowered, they can be powerful agents of change, both for themselves and for their communities.

As Kanyashree Prakalpa moves forward, it will be important to build on the program's successes and to address the challenges that it still faces. By increasing funding, expanding the reach of the program, strengthening implementation, addressing structural issues, and improving evaluation, Kanyashree Prakalpa can continue to be a leading force for gender equality in India and beyond.

The success of Kanyashree Prakalpa demonstrates that, with the right support and resources, girls can achieve great things. By investing in the education and empowerment of girls, we can create a brighter future for all.

9 798889 862345

Printed by Libri Plureos GmbH in Hamburg,
Germany